AFTER SEYMOUR'S FUNERAL

AFTER
SEYMOUR'S FUNERAL

Roy McFadden

**THE
BLACKSTAFF
PRESS**

BELFAST

11/12/90

First published in 1990 by
The Blackstaff Press Limited
3 Galway Park, Dundonald, Belfast BT16 0AN, Northern Ireland
with the assistance of
The Arts Council of Northern Ireland

Typeset by Textflow Services Limited

Printed by the Guernsey Press Company Limited

British Library Cataloguing in Publication Data

McFadden, Roy 1921–
After Seymour's funeral.
1. Title
821.912

ISBN 0-85640-434-9

CONTENTS

BED AND BREAKFAST

Daybreak recalls, informs the furniture;
While, *sotto voce*, silhouettes repair
To church, with book and handkerchief, to pray.
Sir: do not put down innocents today.

Morning's a woman who comes in to pull
Back curtains, open up the vestibule;
To put out aspidistras in the sun,
And tell the resident gong the day's begun.

You'll make yourself at home, love, here; but know
To keep your baggage packed, prepared to go.

THE INNOCENT EYE

The cottages at Ballyhackamore,
For instance, or
Houses with names, before the builders came –
Demolished, vanished now –
Stage properties in an eternity
Of childhood rubbing shoulders with the scene,
Seem rather, in recall,
Actors, directors, sentient presences,
As time and place, in retrospect, stand still.

Vanished; usurped by structures no one loves,
No exile mourns.
But wait; for here and there about the town –
Behind veneers, facades,
On gable-walls at corners, or unmasked
By bulldozer or bomb – you may discern
Pale skeletons
Of family names, antique advertisements,
Obscured or elbowed-out before your time.

So, somewhere in the suburbs of the mind,
Landmarks remain;
And, if you're constant, the familiar
Timeless fraternity
Will hold your gaze against unaltered skies,
That shepherded the living and the dead,
When you were told
That the departed never travelled far
Beyond belief, or doubted their recall.

HYDE PARK

Memorialising trees
Interpret light to dark.
Ducks on the Serpentine
Usher like offspring consequential wakes.
Still, hands in pockets, pigeons steal the scene.

What memory filched, misquotes,
Challenges context now.
The retrospective view
Of parkland and the skyline's pokerwork,
If ever a quotation, now quotes you.

Take heed of that fabulous boy,
Immortalised in stone,
Trapped in a ring nearby;
Commanding shadows, adjuring distances:
His forward gesture pointing to yesterday.

THE DANCERS, SLOANE STREET

for Margaret

Unlike the statues round the City Hall –
    Hand on lapel or heart –
    They partner light and air,
    The diffident shadows of leaves;
Still-lives, exempt from the ephemeral
    Moment which they portray:
    As, time checked in its stride,
    They stand fullstretched like a wave
Apple-laden with sun before its fall.

Alone in their enclave, among the trees
    Hedged in a private green,
    Their slow grave ecstasy
    Takes, gives back solitude:
Yet, casual strangers, taken by surprise,
    Observe them and rejoice,
    And summon to the mind
    Appropriate music; and,
Behind a cough, the notes materialise.

So many glances, if you think of it,
    May leave their signature –
    Like tatters on a bush
    Crouched at a holy well –
So, when you look, you may reactivate
    Head-over-shoulder eyes,
    Transient messengers
    Saying remember me:
Past, present, future stilled by those dancing feet.

THE HILL

Hard in the cold night air,
Their cries tumbled and rang,
Commanding, over the snow, downhill
To where I guarded my circle of light, enthralled:
Rang; and then, as it were,
Catching their breath, ran echoing back uphill.

Careless of frigid gloves
And starved, snow-heavy feet,
The girls laughed; and the flighty light,
Flirting with slides in their hair, obliquely glanced
At shadows miming love's
Flight and pursuit through trees in the trembling night;

Until the housemaid called:
When, whispering, they went in,
Their laughter thorned on an icicle;
And, yes, that music, suddenly aware,
Missed the connection, stalled;
And the snowball flinched in my hand, at the foot of the hill.

Prim midday, sober-eyed,
Restored the Newcome girls,
A shade withdrawn, superior,
To their milieu of stylish cars that took
The hillside in a stride;
The redhaired maid they'd brought from Manchester.

It never once recurred,
That cold lucid delight,
Swept up with childhood; not until,
Rooting through cupboards, limiting excess,
I saw again, and heard,
Those silhouettes, their voices, on the hill.

THE STUFFED FOX

for Victor Kennedy

His presence under the trees,
Rippling with shadows, combed
By amber fingers of sun:
For a moment he stands alone, testing the air,
Ears up, guessing the mood of quirky grass,
 Joint-cracking stones in the ditch,
 A bored shrub's petulance;
Rooted, yet tensed to spring, life honed to kill,
Peripheral, a shady customer;
 The taut nerve of the place.

Now, dressed to kill, he stands,
 A stiffened attitude,
 Collector's bric-a-brac,
An undemanding pet for room or hall;
And, as they carry out the merchandise
 Towards the sun-baked car,
 I say: o countryside,
Predators, victims, acquiescent gods,
Shake leaves, crack twigs, bend grass, in memory
 Of his immaculate stride.

A DEAD CHIEF

An old man, pondering by my desk,
Deferring to professional advice,
Suddenly kindled into poetry,
And cupped an ear in retrospect
To where, facing the class, he'd squared his voice
To grapple with Gray's *Elegy*;
Or hushed and rounded it
In reverence for *The Lady of Shalott*:

In a golden apple-county. Where,
Within a twelve-month (still, he'd have said, on course)
He came back to his parish and its dead;
And left, befittingly for one
With a chief's ticket, all his late affairs
Properly logged, shipshape; godspeed
Ahead, past distances
And voyages becalmed in his spent eyes:

Ashore with the buoyant dead. Where, yes,
Young apple-trees held blossoms in their arms,
Across the hedges, in memoriam.
But I held back to hear the sea,
Where, after hectic nights and days of storms,
He'd calm the panting engine, climb
To sluice himself with stars,
And turn the wind's head with a gust of verse.

JACK YEATS AT FITZWILLIAM SQUARE

Just as, when books were scarce during the war,
   You bought, and set aside
   For less demanding times,
These secondhand, disowned originals,
But never found a proper time, till now,
   Dusting the shelves, to hunker down
With household names the house first came to know
   Years, no, decades ago:

So you reserved and shelved that afternoon
   Until another time
   Elected, overleaf,
To re-enact the scene; with you aside,
Prompting, or undemonstrative, above
   With the celestial audience;
Yet recognising the young actor who
   Purported to be you.

War in the North. In Dublin, undoused streets,
   The neutral tricolour.
   And, in Fitzwilliam Square,
The relics of old decency and style
Glimpsed through a window or a door ajar;
   Where talk drew up an easy chair
In public places; and young Dedalus
   Glanced from a passing bus.

Gracious, benign, the old man raised a hand;
   Murmuring, bowed and smiled.
   Egyptian cigarettes:
A choice of sherry, medium, sweet, or dry.
Throughout, sporadic knocking at the door:
   Discreetly deprecating hands
Conferring some mundane necessity;
   A murmured courtesy.

So, as when taking down a book you find
  A letter interleaved,
  Embalmed for twenty years,
And read, with hindsight, what's between the lines:
Discarding all the famous faces there,
  Mature reflection indicates,
Within those giving hands, framed in the door,
  A kind of metaphor.

CARRIE COATES

Unwilling to shake hands,
For fear of germs she said,
She rummaged in her skirt
For a man's handkerchief
To dust the hooded armies off the chair.

Raw meal and orange juice
Sustained her. She discerned
A light upon my brow,
And murmured that AE
Would have endorsed my juvenilia.

She brought them home like strays,
My mother, in from the cold,
To stretch their hands to the fire;
To muse, and prophesy.
And they were always old, obsessed, and wise.

A name in his letters now –
An eager girl, she said –
If pressed, she might have told
Whether her mentor saw
More than reflections in her broaching eyes.

Their close platonic walks
Among God's metaphors
Kept to the higher ground;
While guts and genitals,
Brute ecstasy and anguish seethed below.

Mick Collins, on the run,
Cut short the monologue;
Stubbed pencil-butt on pad
Jammed on his knee, and said:
Your point now, Mr Russell, if you please.

A crone in a picture-book,
Consigned to the gloryhole
With old, discarded toys:
Nevertheless, she still
Cranes from a chair, intent on the heart of the fire.

THE UPANISHADS

She hadn't known, she said,
A solitary prayer
Before she went to school.
The Lord's Prayer, she declared,
Was something she picked up
In kindergarten, when
Peekaboo infants held –
Familiar, nonchalant –
Their tête-à-tête with God.

I taught you one, I said,
Of the Upanishads,
Put into English by
Shree Purchit Swami for
The poet William Yeats
To hammer out the words –
As Blake, so Yeats averred,
Hammered upon the wall
Till truth obeyed his call.

We send them out with a kiss,
A name and a handkerchief;
But fail to school them in
The qualifying smile,
The double negative;
The last stand not too far
From bridges still unburned:
And how to say *Gosh* when
All other words have failed.

DETAIL FOR A PAINTING

for Alan Seaton

Posterity, I said,
Would not be troubled if he got it wrong.
A wall demolished forty years ago
Was not likely to haunt
Even a wistful resident
Turning his car where ivy used to grow;
The gateway in residual brick,
The pathway to the introverted glens,
Choked by a cul-de-sac.

Nevertheless, he dwelt
On angle, line of brick and copingstone,
Roofshadow, stables mouldering in the gloom;
And held up each unsought
New adumbration to the light –
The cottage-flowers, the trees – as if for some
Adjudicator who would rule
Which revelation merited a place
On some celestial wall.

He worked to repossess,
Pursuing colour, shadow, angle, line –
As well as likenesses, an atmosphere,
A commonplace of joy,
An early-morning certainty;
Evenings agog, with perfume in the air –
As if, redressing place and time,
He could erase the cul-de-sac's dead-end,
And finally draw home.

JUNE BLOSSOM

Ramore Head, summertime;
Fort of the hinterland.
Breakers below, beating their linen white
On foaming rocks. Swing low, to indicate
The recreation grounds:
Grazing for bowlers, nets
For dancing butterflies. *Advantage out;*
Ah, too much green. The gulls
Wheedle, expostulate.
And, out of sight, reportedly ahead,
Apocryphally latent in the mist,
A word: America.

And, also down below,
Bleached by Atlantic gales,
That shack once opened up those blistered doors
To deckchairs and the groundlings on the hill.
Then a precarious troupe
Of summer troubadours
Suffered the sleekit drizzle of July:
June Blossom's Company
Of Laughter, Song & Dance –
A household, no, a boarding-household name –
Versed in the skit, the sketch, the monologue;
Seasoned professionals.

Upstaged by a hot sun,
Or fly, gatecrashing winds,
They played for sticky pennies, and the few
Sixpences from deckchair affluence.
They were a catchy tune
Drowning the gravel voice
Of gavel-thumping sea; a parasol
Flouting predicted rain;

A rainbow's amnesty.
So, when she walked out shopping in the town,
People stopped short, and lingered to engage
   And memorise her smile.

SUNDAY-SCHOOL EXCURSION

She, whom boys pursued
Because of her blue eyes,
Her jaunty step and swinging hair,
He said: framed in the carriage window, blazed
And beat boys from the door.
And, ruefully remembering, said:
You were the chosen gallant at her side.

And thought me close or coy
When I incredulously
Smiled my disclaimer, and instead
Remembered races on the beach, and then
The cinematograph,
Biscuits and yellow lemonade;
Scuffles and giggles while the curate prayed.

But, unflushed until now,
The buoyant memory's
Of her companions whispering,
Wet-luscious-lipped from Tropical Delights,
How, in the wilderness,
God's outcast, excommunicant,
For want of manna, kneaded excrement.

NIGHT OUT

– When, like wafers of peat in the grate,
The conversation wavers and falls,
You summon to heel
Performances, pocket your anecdotes,
And covertly feel
For the hard ringed finger, mate of the sleeping lock.
– Then, singled out by the night,
Resist new turnings, sounds in the stopped town
With its refuse of footprints, appointments, bereft
Greetings and gestures in doorways, looks leaning against walls,
And the voice that says go back, begin again.
– And, pledging another time, reclaim
The familiar shapes in the hall, a stair's *qui vive*,
The curtain drawn on the garden forgetting its lines.
And, stepping down shingle through shallows to shelving sleep,
Humble the heart, and pray,
After your fashion, your small talk bundled away –
Like an unknown guest at a party, alone with his glass –
For a distant nod from the host, an acknowledging smile.

IDYLL

Early October, say –
A premonition of frost – when trees
Were personal elegies; and new
Nights of shadows, close, peripheral,
Shunning the lamplight, hurriedly
Eschewed, it might have seemed,
Tremors of footsteps avenues away.

You listened too, you said,
During those breathless evenings,
Not for an anxious bark in the hills
Or upbraiding strands of laughter from Strandtown,
But for the tip of toes and tap
Of tell-tale heels, a lisp
Of skirt; the handbag rhythmic on her hip.

And when her shadow passed
(Itself scented, you swore) – lamplight
Unmasking vivid cheek and hair –
Then, catching breath, you said, you memorised,
Obscurely between love and lust,
Not the banality
Of flesh; but style: indifferent and chaste.

PIM

A character in corduroy,
  With knitted tie or silk cravat,
He said his father had known Oscar Wilde.
  Employed, sporadically,
  In bookshops, he'd dissuade
A customer from some expensive choice,
  And recommend instead
  A shilling paperback.
Pressed, he'd quote Baudelaire and Mallarmé.

  Part-time performer at the Arts,
  He was a born professional
In playing every character as Pim.
  Not least, his private parts
  In codpiece, scrotum-tight,
(*The Lady's not for Burning*) ridiculed
  The bridle and the bit.
  He gathered up applause
Like hothouse flowers he'd nurtured in their hearts.

  And, annotating library
  Borrowings with his mandarin style,
Commending, reprimanding, he'd extend
  Essays and homilies
  To margins and fly-leaves,
Seducing errant readers from the text;
  And, in that way, survives –
  Attached to literature –
A prompter in the wings, a telling voice.

THE FOSTER TWINS

Tell how the Foster twins,
  Equally beautiful,
Fair hair goldgrained, braided with sun,
Leading the little foxes down the hill
Past squiring hedges and obeisant trees
  – Unblinking yellow eyes
  Of cats lighting the leaves –
  Stepped from a marvellous sky,
Braced on the slope against the tightening leash.

Not old enough to share
  In casual ribaldry,
Mimetic gestures, elbow-talk,
I breathed in their magnificence like scent
Encountered in a garden late at night –
  Not quite a moon, but light
  Seeping back from the west –
  When sudden ecstasy
Confronts, adjures, rejects, and backs away.

THE INVISIBLE MENDERS

Hailing the daily miracle,
Expectant on the stairs or at the door –
Invisibility made manifest –
He beckoned, as the raucous girls
Trooped from their attic down to the tart air.

But one was so exceptional
That her translucent skin, those brilliant eyes,
Insinuated signals of decline.
She's not long for this world. Aside,
The old wives ostracised her otherness.

She vanished. To another job,
McKelvey said; had married; or, who knows,
Perhaps the wagging heads had got it right.
Soon afterwards, her absence filled
And sank beneath those grosser presences.

When, after winter, she appeared,
McKelvey, hand on heart, behind the door,
Cried out *Persephone*; but, softly, said
The flush, the lowered look, implied
No one would make a job of mending her.

GALLAGHER'S DONKEY

for William and Mary Galbraith

Aware of us, she comes
Out of the covert air
With evening in her eyes,
Docile, ineffably resigned
To silences, acceptances;
And lifts her muzzle to the nudging hand

Clumsy with peppermints:
His gruff, even grotesque,
Token of love for her
Dependence and her diffidence;
While evening's bright perimeter,
Nearing eclipse, is at its most intense.

Securing gates, recall
That midnight, when we heard
From under the young trees
A cry wrung out of solitude,
Moved for a moment to surmise
God's voice is a harsh grief in a dark wood.

THE LITTLE BLACK ROSE

To whom shall I bequeath the wooden bowl,
Engraved with twelve wild roses, rimmed
  With Celtic lettering?
  How glibly I spelt out
The coded language of the parable –
Oracular, like something they had dreamed –
  While they stood, listening.

They chanted back the words. *It will*, they said,
Redden the hills when June is nigh;
  And new affinities,
  A latent idiom,
Sweetened, and called out from the countryside
Beyond the gardens and the motorway,
  To stir familial trees.

But blood, stark on the street, cries louder than
A sentimental metaphor.
  A manic Irishry
  Has crudely paraphrased
Romance in monologues of bomb and gun;
And girls in black bring white clenched rosebuds for
  Red tumuli of clay.

I gave them Irish names; but I'll bequeath,
Salvaging words from rhetoric –
  The black, infected rose
  A captive emblem now
For self-ordained hot-gospellers of death –
What I inherited: a maverick
  Integrity; a voice.

MEMORY OF SAND

The pierrots gone, an end-of-season sea
Sweeps up the summer's leavings. A derelict wind
Has requisitioned shelters on the hill
Where he, so lately, stood to view,
Behind the islands shipshape for the night,
The shrinking boats depart;
While, privately, his disengaging blood
Prepared its own goodbyes.

Romantic word that lacks a synonym,
O heart, recalcitrant heart: the scattering light's
Sharp ricochet from a dark afterthought
Catches a look-out on the hill,
Now you have turned a summer holiday
Into a pilgrimage
To where young children's castles on the strand
Held sway between the tides.

THERE AND BACK

I walked out with my grandfather,
  Great with chattering hedges, trees –
Survivors since before the builders came –
Loopholes and coigns of nettles, buttercups
And dandelions, rampant, rural still;
  I with his past; my years ahead
  Latent for him in leaf's lipcurl
And undermist of trees: o, hand in hand,
His fathers and my children ventured through
A child's slow afternoon, whose distances
  Promised, but said take time;
  And faraway catastrophes
Lazed on the sidelines, not as yet on call.

The plumtree's vanished; but the hedge,
  Long in my keeping, quickens still.
Lamp-posts are gone, and most of Stringer's trees;
And, here and there, new doors, brash parvenus,
Fail to acclimatise; but everywhere –
  Laurel and privet, bread-and-cheese –
  Old dogged hedges prick up ears.
I hear the caught breath of that afternoon,
An afterthought of place surviving time;
And, conscious of the crowding distances
  Saying take care, beware,
  I call a child back to explain
The silence that contains my grandfather.

AFTER SEYMOUR'S FUNERAL

I

They tidy papers, retrospectively
Put lives in order. I have made out Herbertson's will,
Spoken of books to Mullan. Monaghan
Has named a college for his manuscripts.
They are busy editing their yesterdays,
Tailoring tall tales for mythology.

I watch their evening stumble into night.

I loathe this decade, but I'll suffer it,
Sinclair asseverates, a cellophane
Sandwich in hand. Herbertson peers, inquires
For prunes in supermarkets. Monaghan,
The blackthorn gangling lamely in the hall,
Commends brown bread, and milk, and oranges.
Mullan reads Flaubert, eating distantly.

They reach out for survival in their words.

2

Herbertson pushed the button. Eighty years
Of Seymour shafted down
Into whatever name
You give to afterwards. His will being done,
He got no hymns or prayers, or obsequies.

Complaisantly,
Herbertson quoted Yeats, for Seymour's sake.
No spade on stone,
No turds of earth, contorted wreaths, or tears.
Someone complained
Down in the car park of the burning leaves.

3

Somebody, sure enough, was moved to say:
He drags a chair, to eavesdrop on the talk
Of Yeats, head-down with Landor and with Donne.
Across the city, sirens chorused round
Laconic murder in the street; who would
Commend *him* to whose hospitality?

Outside T. Just the Grocer's, decades past,
A younger Seymour fingered his cravat.
The rain falls on T. Just and T. Unjust.
Grace, Thoreau said, not justice. Summer then.
Butterfly sunlight. The young year in love.
Peach-blossom on an old tenacious wall.

4

White crosses on the lawn
Facing the City Hall,
The widow's ritual
Of camera-conscious grief,
Epitomise a town
Where death's a cliché and a way of life.

The river, underground,
Heaves shoulders for release;
Low-flying back to base,
Surveillant gulls pick out
Middens of rubble, and
A slumped abandoned bundle on the street.

5

Buildings, as well, are citizens.
In this bad town
They have shut up shop, closed eyes and ears; are dumb.
Touch wood and stone.
Linger in hallways; eavesdrop on the stairs.

Nothing responds; your whisper dies at your feet.
This morning, the buried river rose in the street.

While sun presumes, and gulls streel in from the lough,
A ruined terrace hangs a heavy head,
Glass whirs and chimes from ragged window-frames.
Today, the insurgent river took over the street.

6

Though we believed, or tried,
The beggars have failed,
Staccato with crutches and cans,
To march on the town;
And screeching gates defer
To drovers herding acquiescent hooves.
Still, though we chose to stay,
The prisons suppurate;
Keepers harassed with keys
Salute, and genuflect
To totem flags and godforsaken spires.
You told us then; and we believed; or tried.
Wait. Wait a little longer. . . They will come.

7

Whatever doors there are,
Wherever bells to ring,
Inquire
What sleep, what absence or forgetfulness
Defaulted or betrayed.
We waited; but, alas,
Apparelled differently,
They came by stealth,
Suborned the crier, commandeered his voice.
Like tolerated dogs, the poets stand
Sad-eyed with greed outside the butchers' shops.

8

Glaziers' hammers in Ann Street
After the patriots' bombs;
Emergency shutters of hardboard
Pre-emptively at hand;
Buses burned in the depots:
A population resigned
To follow the ruts that tumbrils
Have totted like debts on the streets.

Wherever – here or there –
Whenever – now or then –
War, you declared,
Is the inverted self
Of mirror-images –
MacTweedledum against McTweedledee –
Whose glib apologists
Make altar-room for flags
Amenably with hymns;
And walk the road with hard
Men clubbing calloused drums.

While patriots infiltrate,
Plain citizens lack language to prefer
A proper challenge at the barricades.
Who, they could say, *goes where?*

Today, they blocked the bridges, the
Traffic festered in the thoroughfares.
Old, abdicating buildings close
Their eyes, hands at their sides, aghast.

While dust recoils
From the smoke's uprising, wounds
Of aching absence let
In profiles of sky and a quizzical eyebrow of birds.

The have tidied bricks into cairns where a terrace died.
Staying is nowhere, Serafico, now.

9

Ask those who ladle out
Their lives in sonnets and pentameters
Who will exclaim bravo
In roofless space above the birthday stars.
Who cries out Author now?
And also ask to know
From addicts of applause,
The impresarios
Saying good show, good show –
The shadow-boxers and
The ukelele-men –
Who answers to the call
Of Reverence for Life
(Conceding Life's a cry
Italicised by death):
Whatever rootless space,
Agnostic or malign –
(The buried river's call) –
Engenders or consigns.

10

Abruptly, I think of him then,
Tweedy and windblown, with the laughing dog,
Alive in summer, at Glencree, among
The young trees near where Joseph Campbell died
Pitched on the hearth, the passing postman warned
By the cold chimney, smokeless in the wind.

11

That bitter-sweet decade; those elegies.
The barren peach-tree on the garden wall
Urgent with blossom when the laughing dog –
Now only I remember – stopped, and died.

HANS CRESCENT

Forgotten phrases, images, recur,
And you identify,
Respond,
As if to messages
Flashed back from outposts in the hinterland.

The day's first-footed by the cavalry.
The Aston-Martin man
Unveils
Immaculate mannequins.
You watch for life in *Town & Country Dogs*;

Where, undeluded by dilating glass,
They gambol narrowly,
Informed
By warmth and nearness. Noon:
Alas, the window's bare; day's come to heel.

PARVENUS

Those who come late to words,
   McKelvey said,
End up possessed. You've noted how
They confiscate another's audience,
The sly cough followed by an anecdote.
   And you'll have watched hard men, seduced
   By personal rhetoric, pursue
Clichés, the drabs of speech, but, in their book,
   Mots justes for every parvenu
Who takes the willing victim by the throat.

Those who come late to fame,
   McKelvey said –
The tailored beard, the jockey-cap,
The open collar and the loose cravat –
End up as prisoners of a posture; and,
   Stopped in the street, they'll hesitate
   Until they haltingly recall
Whose hand it is you shake, as if afraid
   A chance remark from you might hale
Back disaffection from the hinterland.

OLD STYLE

She was extremely small; not more
  Than four-foot-six I guessed.
And she was also fabulously old,
A Queen Victoria in rusty black:
  Commanding a café table, or
Clasping her books in Donegall Square West.

Held high, a babe in arms, she said
  She'd witnessed Wellington's
Imperial funeral march. An uncle sat
In Grattan's Parliament at College Green.
  She'd peddled tea to pay her dues
And lived on air, to graduate from Queen's.

As later, when I knew her, she
  Lunched off a penny bun,
Saving a guinea for the library.
And, penny-pinching, resolutely skimped
  On tram-fares, and was seen to tramp
Enormous distances, shrunk in the rain.

Despite her foreign languages,
  She said demurely – Greek,
And French, and English – nonetheless, she cried,
She was illiterate in her native tongue.
  Each day, at noon, she'd meditate
On Ireland, closed and still behind her book.

Descended from Ascendancy,
  She'd chosen to pursue
An unprotected path outside the pale.
Irish, not *Anglo-Irish*, she decreed.
  At noon today, compatriots,
One with a gun, gutted the library.

OLD KNOCK GRAVEYARD

These are our dead, he called,
Nodding concurringly,
Flaunting accommodating arms;
Then laughed to indicate
The mimicry. *These are our dead*,
He said again, and stroked
A stone with local names in copperplate.

But they do not belong.
Touching a stone, pronounce
Gelston, or *Kelly of Strandtown*;
Turn leaves aside to note
The dates, the lifespan and the text.
Those knowing witnesses,
Hoarding the years, the watchful trees, are mute.

Ours only in the sense
That *we* are the possessed.
As, fused by darkness, branches turn
Bright palms up to the sun –
Survivors and interpreters –
So, housing ousted lives,
We hold a door against oblivion.

MY MOTHER'S YOUNG SISTER

A new decade, the teacher cried,
Clapping chalk from her hands.
Then: *1930*. Someone laughed
Uncertainly; the rest of us were awed.

By 1939 we'd be
Coping with Life, she said.
Did I hold back a thought for you
Trapped in the Twenties, young Persephone?

My youth, not yours, is stirred again
By summer photographs,
Items of Twentyish furniture,
That outfaced decades you have never known.

But, in sleep's undertone, you came,
Sidestepping memory,
Vivid, vivacious; unperturbed
By futures come and gone after your time.

And I caught at your perfume, and
Half-heard the teacher say
You are a shade too old for him:
Above my head, as though *you'd* understand.

But such discrepancy in years
Death stands upon its head:
You, twenty-three for ever now,
My age careering towards my grandfather's.

You were a girl who hurried past
My childhood, with a dream's
Inconstancy; as if forewarned,
Time being short, you had to travel fast.

A SMALL INCIDENT IN TOWN

Rejecting her containing hand –
   Defecting, breaking free –
He dared the artful dodgers (chance, mischance)
Idling at corners, weighing circumstance;
   While, shepherding clouds, the sky
Swept on regardless, turning a blind eye.

Well-heeled insurgent on the run,
   Elbowing through the crowd,
He yearned for one upstanding citizen's
Conspiratorial concurring glance,
   Another solitude
Stooping to his, showing it understood.

Then, as the traffic's hue and cry
   Smothered his way across
To exile somewhere off Victoria Square,
Morosely turning, he caught sight of her
   Eyes, vivid as a voice:
The motherland of her abandoned face.

A MAN OBSERVED STANDING BESIDE A GRAVE

Frowning, as if he doubts
The grave's identity,
His face in profile lowers
Over the laundered earth;
Exhuming ages, dates,
Reflects on family
Connections, disconnections, feuds, amours,
Some sudden death and compensating birth.

Looking again, I see,
Instead, what's obvious,
That he's engaged in prayer;
Set piece, or personal
Avowal; a late plea
For clemency. Or is
He standing up with all the headstones there
Calling on God to be accountable?

THE STATUTE OF LIMITATIONS

A boy, hunched from the rain,
 Running to meet me, arms aslant
To house the young dog bosomed in his coat
From streeling trees and hedges, cradled it
 With such compassionate
Commitment (call it love) and wonderment

That, all these decades on,
 His future coffined with my past –
Your first sorrow, my mother said, when I
Put on my Sunday suit, with a black tie –
 The moment's poignancy
Confronts me like a scar, vivid, aghast.

Why tell, or try to tell?
 Custodian of absences,
Attorney, self-appointed, I declare
An interest, here and now, in then and there;
 And speak up to defer
The statute running out for absentees.

OLD TENNIS COURTS

A rueful connoisseur
Of relics – such as old
Forsaken tennis courts, usurped
By upstart, coarser grass,
Trespassing branches trailing elegies
Across where evening sunlight sauntered past
Tableaux of white and green –
He could, he said, relate
Their message to the death
Of (call it) elegance or style
In being, doing, art,
Quotidian once, he said, as sun or rain:
The actors glimpsed among attentive trees,
The picture's discipline.

From memory he restores
The blurred particulars;
Paints in the figures, white on green,
Engaged in play, the trees,
Branches inched back, showing a greener leaf;
The ambling sunlight lingering on the side,
Suspending disbelief:
While I, toeing the line
Under the specious grass,
Address the hidden court and call
Upon a silhouette,
Rallying back to credibility,
To pair the faltering present with the past,
Contemporaneously.

FOR THE RECORD

Herbertson telephoned:
In need of someone old enough, he said,
To put back into context incidents
That happened in our time,
Which hearsay garbles and misrepresents.

A sharp American
Cocked his recorder for the interview;
Unloaded questions. *You and I were there*,
I mocked; and Herbertson
Sagely concurred, and trimmed his smouldering briar.

Identity; degree
Of Irishness; the label on the jar.
Backed by his books, the old man underlined
I am of Planter stock.
A ring of smoke endorsed his nodding hand.

Planter and Gael. Estranged
From both the new grim Irish and the old
Colonial retrospection, I held forth
Over the scurrying tape.
When I was a barefoot lad in the English North.

GRAND OLD MAN

After a lifetime of neglect,
Honours, like conscience-money, dividends
Long overdue,
Slide from the table to the floor,
Prop open doors; or stand like jovial cards
Saying get well.

He mounts the medals, catalogues
The portraits, caskets and certificates,
The sculpted head;
Complains that freedom of the town
Does not extend to transport. Erinmore
Costs just the same.

And, taken in at last, aspires
To be a doyen among younger men,
Fount more than shrine,
Who hump his harp to parties, laud
His patience, prudence and sagacity,
His sturdy style.

But, late at night, in dishabille –
The metal fire cold comfort in the grate;
An empty chair –
He raises retrospective eyes
Up to an earlier portrait, done for love,
And tells it all.

WILLIAM COWPER

Being damned,
He stopped longing for meaning, or
Mooning towards the stars. The readymade
Pattern of life – he extended his hands – is here.

Debarred,
No longer banking on paradise,
He cashed each day's remittances
For instant use against immediacies.

It wasn't that
He'd bartered his salvation for
Pleasure or privilege; condemned,
Credulity obliged him to concur

And pass the time –
Winter without hope of spring –
Shin-deep in endings, torn-up leaves,
Composing hymns for simple souls to sing.

THREE COUSINS

I
The Day of the May Queen

Exile returned, disguised
With an alien accent and
A married name: Cousin,
Let me re-create and restore
To you the skipping-games
In the street, the swing, and the songs;
The sense of forever under
The streetlamp's widening
Benignly censorious eye and outstretched arms.

Never the queen, you sighed,
You were always a step behind,
Attending, adjusting her train.
Now – queen of your own domain –
In this forsaken town,
You're moved to abdicate,
And quicken step again
To bask in that other's shade,
Lady-in-waiting courting summer still.

2
The Kodak Kid

'Shy in my Sunday best,'
She said, 'I peeped to where
You read, chin propped on wrist,
Sleep-postured on the floor:

My age, and beautiful;
And unapproachable.

'A chemist's shop in the town
Displayed a cardboard boy
With camera, eyes cast down
As if in reading. I,
Minding that private view,
Posed in the street for you.'

3
The Other Grandfather

A shying horse; a flying rein.
Clattering yardmen ran
To lift the traveller in, and softly swore
As, deprecatingly,
Blood curdled like coarse spittle on the floor.
Dying, he journeyed home again,
Across the river and its daffodils,
And heard, from the cathedral, through the whin,
Long spades strike stones, like bells.

Let's say an anxious child ran out
To ask the time of day;
The weathered saints on the cathedral wall,
The old saint's sepulchre,
Appeared to listen; and the prescient bell,
Clearing its throat, stood by to play
Its modest repertoire for funerals;
A young apprentice, dawdling in the street,
Hearkened for harness-bells.

You delve for dates. I speculate.
But I presumed to add

The name omitted from the monument,
After – what? – eighty years.
Though no one quotes a single incident,
One mortal word he ever said,
Yet, picture how, in passing, a young blade –
Ages before you set out in pursuit –
Cousin, inclined your head.

HOUSE UNDER CONSTRUCTION

Eleven or so, drifting on wheels
Under the cherry-trees, a mile
Or so out of my bailiwick,
In a parish of blossoms, pink and white like girls,
I skirted a spillage of sand, ladders aloft,
Hodsmen, like firemen, shouldering virgin brick:
Cavities, waiting to smile,
Addressing a prospect of doors and window-glass,
Appendant to coming and going, ingress, egress.

My house. Not yet; but, marking time
Assured of my advent. Had I
Been told, would I have turned to look
For the stranger cutting the grass, tending the car;
Or for children, perhaps, under the cherry-trees,
Running, or drifting on wheels; the weathered brick
Benign? Or, free to pry
Beyond to a cruel end, still marking time,
Have dared to sign the contract just the same?

THE ROCKERY

My father built a rockery
To mask the gulley-trap;
Embroidered it with snow-in-summer, and
Enclosed an underworld
Where I addressed a child's credulity
Not to the motive but the mystery,
A tongue-tied oracle;
Where revelation waited for a word
Which I had still to learn.

Pasts hibernate. Their dreams
Infiltrate memory.
A ladybird enamelled on a tree;
Evening: a gramophone
Heard by a child in bed while murmuring
Lawnmowers groomed the grass; my mother's voice
Rehearsing a new song;
Tweed and tobacco fragrance when I seized
My father's homeward hand.

Just as when, then, I stared full-eyed
Into the underworld,
The wooden horse abandoned in the hedge,
So, in these later years,
Going back home, I conjure houses, trees,
As if the suburb were a rockery,
Where childhood, closed inside,
Secreted like a helpless oracle,
Will not come out to tell.

THE BAR LIBRARY

The anteroom, McKelvey improvised,
   Is their forecourt; or, say,
   A neutral interface
   With actuality:
Where, nonchalant without the wig and gown,
   Their order's uniform –
   Plainsuited nuncios,
Fraternal, man-to-man, colloquial –
   They take in custody
Gauche inconsistent truths, so help them God.

Sometimes (he rocked the promise in his arms)
   You'll get a baby one –
   Lamb's wig, a too-big gown,
   Sixth-former's awkward scrawl –
And hold his hand in court, ventriloquise
   Words to placate his lord;
   And later, in the pub,
Toasting a win or drowning a defeat –
   The fee marked on the brief –
Recoil from future judgments in his eyes.

THE SILVERMAN PLEA

The pleas were always taken first:
Succinctly, without argument;
Then strictures from the bench; the penalty.
We cynical conveyancers,
Used to a different discipline,
Said slot-machines would cope as readily.

But that's forgetting Silverman.
His plea was Guilty-but. Impassively
Unrolling mitigating circumstance –
Reneging on admitted facts –
He'd finally insinuate
A covert case of injured innocence.

Behind the sweetening courtesies –
With great respect; If it may please the Court –
We read the blasphemous argument,
As he defensively arraigned
A wider culpability,
That facts themselves are seldom innocent.

MR McALONEN

The raincoat, bowler-hat
And solemn spectacles
Betokened a head clerk
In Ewart's or the Ropeworks, or perhaps
Some kind of major-domo, seneschal,
To family merchants in Victoria Street:
    A liberal Methodist.
He played bowls in the park on summer nights;
    At home, grew lettuces,
And made a pleasance from suburban grass.

Always dependable
To brave the elements
For meetings and debates,
He sat, impassive, inarticulate,
Impregnable behind his spectacles.
Good afternoon, for him, was eloquence.
    Familiar furniture
At meetings, we moved round him, talked across
    His woollen cardigan;
But marked his absence after he had gone.

So, when he took his stand
In Royal Avenue,
Stood up to witness *No*
Against the uniforms, the hangers-on,
The munching, acquiescent citizens,
He suffered insult and indignity
    With such an unconcern
That, huddled with my protest on the kerb,
    I cupped my wavering flame
Behind his unassailable aplomb.

EMIGRANTS

Some I recalled from when,
As if making their vows
Together, hand in hand,
They signed, and touched the seal
On lease and counterpart;
After I had explained, defined
The awkward words, and made a paraphrase,
Acceptably banal,
In substitution for the draftsman's art.

Since when, as vendors – names,
A stylish signature –
Knowing their way around
Life's hereditaments:
Vendors indeed – not just
Of *Chez Nous, Shancoduff*, they signed
Away the past like bits of furniture:
A springtime's muniments
Of title handed over with the rest.

If, as I said goodbye,
Or waved from the stairhead
To faces poised below,
Regret played a slow air
From under a hitched-up sleeve,
All that is past; for gladly now,
With terror's tumbrils uninhibited,
I guide each signature
On instruments that signify reprieve.

THREE CATS

I
A Certain Death

Those mornings when I came down
To darkness and cinders, there,
Its green gaze on the sill
For opening curtains and
The first act of the day,
The histrionic cat
Banked smouldering demands.

My daughter held a hand
Up tearfully in school
To save a kitten from
Death's casual orderlies.
It never licked a hand
Or favoured milk, or sang
Pursed by a settled fire.

Less pet than furniture,
Never identified
With anything except
Its own chair wigged with fur,
A somnolent judge that eyed
Family proceedings with
A cool reserved contempt:

It disdained me the least.
I gave her liver and
White chicken-meat, and then
Knelt conversationally
Caressing head and paws

Till mutilating claws
Punctured pretentious wrists.

Barn cat, uncivilised,
She trusted the vet's hand
And looked with faint surprise
At the bared needle, and
Nobody cried, but yet –
Whenever I come down
To flash the curtains back –

I look outside for her
Intent uncertainty,
Or listen to the tree;
And, unclaimed, hesitate,
Grief retrospectively
Dishonouring relief,
To activate the day.

2
Young Cat in a Hedge

The frightened cat in the hedge:
Not just immaculate fear,
But an outlaw's wariness
Of breathless bushes or
Hushed undulations of grass;
And, masked by trees, a rigid wind as it were,
The presence of the executioner.

The young fox-terrier,
Your earliest love, put down,
The sun wrenched from your sky;
And that barn-creature none

53

But you could pacify,
Bearing the needle's thrust with knowing eyes:
Include, among thrusting thorns, in this one's face.

For one and all now, kneel,
This time to repossess,
Manhandle back to you
From trespass and impasse,
A fox-faced kitten, who,
Across gatecrashing distances, weeps for
The length of a lawn with the door to the house ajar.

3
Elegy for a Friend

Life, or whatever, closed a door;
And, suddenly, with landmarks gone,
You feared your friend, the dark. Those nine
Lives, did all of them combine
To bow out with your uncontracting sigh?
This morning, fittingly, let no dog bark.

An epicure of silence, **sleep** –
Shrewd connoisseur of **fireglow**, sun
On rug and windowsill – o let
Recalled warmth make a coverlet
For your last sleep under the rowan tree
Each time the garden turns to find you gone:

Or when, comrade of earliest days,
Playmate indeed, protector too –
Recalling, later, dignity,
Forbearance, love – faced by a tree
Beyond your climbing now, I bend to say
The garden grows in memory of you.

EVICTIONS

for Padraic Fiacc

Precocious refugee,
Between the ghettoes' fires,
I stopped my tricycle.
A baby in a pram
Held out his penny flag.
I took it. In exchange,
I closed his fingers round
My wooden tomahawk.
On his side, and on mine,
The houses rocketed.
And detonating streets
Clapped reprobating hands:
Exclamatory, like squibs
Let loose on Hallowe'en,
Once thought to exorcise –
Out of the hooded dark –
Demonic messengers
Tending the torch's glow,
The flame's dilating eye,
Eager for holocaust.

THE LITTLE B.A.

My mother called him that;
One of a numinous company
Of unfamilial names
Still vibrant from her meetings. Then,
My father, marking his page, sat back
To smile at her mimicry
Over the warming pot, while her playback
Of lecture and debate offhandedly
Recaptured style and accent to a T.

Urbane and sociable,
Seldom forthright, familiar,
He found congenial ground
In crumbling Georgian premises
Downtown, in dead or dying squares,
Where, ready volunteer
With lectures on AE and Allingham,
He'd flex his elegant phrases, debonair,
Succinct and polished; and particular.

At séances, he said –
A casual fellow-traveller –
He was seduced, possessed
By female voices; sceptical,
He'd lisp falsetto to his friends.
You told me in the car,
After the funeral, of the irony
Of mutilating death in a wheelchair
For one so dapper and particular.

Do you remember a
Letter to William Allingham?
'You heard me speak of one
Lauret, a painter. He is dead.

His watchings, love of nature, toil;
   O all his aspirations – I'm
So grieved; I don't like death, I tell you – dead,
Wiped off the palette, smudged out like a dream.
Four fir-boards. Listen; that's what left of him.'

CAPTAIN THOMPSON

You may contrive, in talking to the dead,
To single out a captive audience
In some abandoned wall, a stranded tree.
   So, when I say thank you
   To Captain Thompson, I
   Will not expect to hear
Modest disclaimers murmured in my ear.

Because he took on board a twelve-year-old
Castaway from two centuries or more
Of clannish forebears, left in the spent town –
   Numbering kith and kin
   From headstones, or the vault's
   Incestuous family tomb –
My father named his firstborn after him.

The old man's only love the open sea –
Passionate, self-consuming, unpossessed –
Aground, he'd trimmed his step to the river's gait;
   His trawling ear withdrawn
   To shallows only of sound;
   The weathered fist on the stick
Eased from the grip that veered past spitting rock.

Born to the craft of Irish Chippendale –
At home with wood, part of the natural grain –
Adrift, a lodger in his family's town,
   My father came to share
   The Captain's table, say
   Amen with him at grace,
And read the morning weather through his eyes.

An aunt said when my father left the town –
Eighteen: hard-collared, tie-pinned – and acquired

(That was her word, acquired) responsible
  Work in a city bank,
  Old Captain Thompson stood,
  Proud tears fierce in his eyes,
To glimpse a silhouette against the glass.

And when he died, she said, without an heir,
My father scorned to ask about a will.
Think of a sea-chest fit to burst, she cried,
  With treasure, maps and things.
  But what he gave, and what
  I celebrate today,
Spilled from a richer, rarer treasury.

Addressing wall or tree, I call to mind
Imperfect, re-created images –
The old man in the street, my father's head
  Clouded by window-glass –
  And shake out speech to find
  Such words of gratitude
As, scattered, may take root among the dead.

GONE AWAY

If I should knock the door and ask for me,
Who would peer past the startled householder,
Over those absent years?
No ghost for sure, from that forever time;
No cupboard skeletons, where candour could
Keep house without locked doors,
Where family entertained a neighbourhood.

Recall the hallstand's station at the door,
The hats and sticks, the mirror's challenging
Or recollecting glance;
The clothesbrush in the drawer with Sunday gloves,
Ancestral prayer-book, old, genteel like lace,
Surviving evidence
Of forebears in a legendary place.

Or say that you're the meter-man, and step
In with authority: nudging at walls
To peel off posthumous paint;
Cajoling carpets to resuscitate
Footprints from smothered wood; conjuring doors
To hark back in complaint,
Under the gloss, to unforgotten scars.

And ask the listening stairs to repossess,
Step at a time, a child climbing to bed,
When, late on Christmas Eve,
Beyond the flashing trams across the trees,
The churches counting blessings in their towers,
Faint sleighbells stretched a sleeve
Of reassurance towards his guttering prayers.

I stroke the hedge, *my* hedge, and turn away,
Back to accessible appearances;

And tell the passing thought
Survival's only in the heart and head.
And yet, if I could earn the missing word,
Such bidden beings might
Smile with relief: seen, seeing; hearing, heard.

OTHER POETRY TITLES

from

THE BLACKSTAFF PRESS

THE LONG EMBRACE
Twentieth-century Irish Love Poems
edited by
FRANK ORMSBY

Tender, passionate, bitter, bawdy, reverential – the poetry of love in Ireland is as various as the lovers and the poets. This anthology presents the best Irish love poems of the twentieth century. Some are uninhibitedly direct, others careful and emotionally circumspect but together they display the sturdiness, the fragility, the transforming power of love in its everyday, familiar settings and circumstances: love as it flourishes – or fails to flourish – in youth and old age, inside and outside marriage; love as a sharing of caresses, love ending in blows; love in time of war; love as it is trammelled by and defies the puritanical dictates of church and state.

Vigorously colloquial or musically formal, rich in imagery or quietly restrained, these poems, selected by the Irish poet Frank Ormsby,

> '. . . record love's mystery without claptrap,
> Snatch out of time the passionate transitory.'

'a very lively and accomplished collection'
Times Literary Supplement

'Every faithful spouse, every licentious rake, every heart-smitten or heart-broken lover should have a copy, preferably on the bedside locker.'
Irish Times

198 x 129 mm; 208 pp; 0 85640 387 3; pb
£6.95

JESUS AND ANGELA
Paul Durcan

Paul Durcan's reputation as an exciting, highly original poet has developed rapidly in recent years with the publication of *The Selected Paul Durcan* (1982), *The Berlin Wall Café* (1985; Poetry Book Society Choice) and *Going Home to Russia* (1987). These three important titles are published by Blackstaff Press and are regularly reprinted to keep pace with the demand generated by Durcan's electrifying poetry readings in Ireland, Britain, Europe, America and Canada.

Many new fans, keen to read all of Durcan's work, have been unable to obtain some of his earlier titles. This book is the author's selection, with revisions, from work originally published in two separate books: *Jesus, Break His Fall* (1980) and *Jumping the Train Tracks with Angela* (1983).

198 x 129 mm; 112 pp; 0 85640 407 1; pb

£5.95

GOING HOME TO RUSSIA
Paul Durcan

'Paul Durcan's. . . collection is, as its title suggests, partly the record of a quest for a spiritual and imaginative home and a celebration of Russia, which the poet visited in 1983 and 1986. Directly and indirectly, the poems on this subject challenge patronising and complacent Western assumptions – both about Russia and the West – and raise questions about the nature of freedom. . .

'*Going Home to Russia* is a substantial collection, the work of an inventive and compassionate poet who continues to surprise and provoke and delight.'

Frank Ormsby, BBC Radio Ulster

'Any new work by Paul Durcan is to be hailed. He is a poet of such power, appeal and vitality that publication is to be eagerly anticipated. *Going Home to Russia* is no exception.'

Martin Booth, *Tribune*

198 x 129 mm; 112; pp; 0 85640 386 5; pb

£4.95

THE BERLIN WALL CAFÉ
Paul Durcan

This startlingly original collection, a Poetry Book Society Choice,
sold out its first and second prints at breakneck speed and
generated unstinted praise from the critics:

'The tenderness, honesty, imaginative daring at work, the generous,
passionate personality which permeates the book, make *The Berlin
Wall Café* the most riveting and moving collection of poems I have read
for some time.'

Belfast Telegraph

'. . . a marvellous collection. There is nothing fragile, exotic or skybrained
about this writing: it has heart and strength, and works in the world we
know.'

Irish News

'What's finally moving in a poem is. . . the channelled pressure of
something being said, the felt knowledge that this is a poem which had to
be written. Paul Durcan's poems bristle with that pressure.'

Irish Times

Poetry Book Society Choice

198 x 129 mm; 80 pp; 0 85640 348 2; pb
£4.95

THE SELECTED PAUL DURCAN
edited by
EDNA LONGLEY

When *The Selected Paul Durcan* first appeared in 1982 the critics
celebrated a unique talent: 'strikingly original. . . a poet to be
reckoned with' (*British Book News*); 'Durcan's irreverent and
iconoclastic vision is a liberating force in contemporary Ireland'
(*Irish University Review*); '[he is] exciting and adventurous. . . as
well as being a writer of real integrity and vision' (*Auditorium*,
BBC); 'he resuscitates one's flagging belief in "the-poet-in-the-
world"' (*Belfast Review*).

Poetry Ireland 1982 Winter Choice

198 x 129 mm; 144 pp; 0 85640 354 7; pb
£4.95

ALL SHY WILDNESS
edited by
ROBERT JOHNSTONE

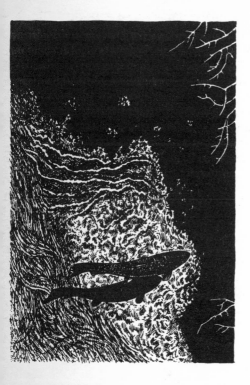

THE TROUT
John Montague

Flat on the bank I parted
Rushes to ease my hands
In the water without a ripple
And tilt them slowly downstream
To where he lay, light as a leaf,
In his fluid sensual dream.

Bodiless lord of creation
I hung briefly above him
Savouring my own absence
Senses expanding in the slow
Motion, the photographic calm
That grows before action.

As the curve of my hands
Swung under his body
He surged, with visible pleasure.
I was so preternaturally close
I could count every stipple
But still cast no shadow, until

The two palms crossed in a cage
Under the lightly pulsing gills.
Then (entering my own enlarged
Shape, which rode on the water)
I gripped. To this day I can
Taste his terror on my hands.

This enchanting anthology presents Irish poems about animals,
birds and insects, by poets ranging from an anonymous
eighth-century monk to Yeats and Heaney. A gift edition, limited
to five hundred copies, quarter-bound in cloth, with matching
slipcase.
    Illustrated by Diana Oxlade.

198 x 129 mm; 84 pp; illus; 0 85640 322 9
£15.00

ORDERING
BLACKSTAFF BOOKS

All Blackstaff Press books are available through bookshops. In the case of difficulty, however, orders can be made directly to the publisher. Indicate clearly the title and number of copies required and send order with your name and address to:

Cash Sales
Blackstaff Press Limited
3 Galway Park
Dundonald
Belfast BT16 0AN
Northern Ireland

Please enclose a remittance to the value of the cover price plus: 60p for the first book plus 30p per copy for each additional book ordered to cover postage and packing. Payment should be made in sterling by UK personal cheque, postal order, sterling draft or international money order, made payable to Blackstaff Press Limited.

Applicable only in the UK and Republic of Ireland
Full catalogue available on request